Dedication

THIS BOOK IS DEDICATED TO MY MOTHER AND FATHER, Joann and Donald Kalajainen. I still can't believe they are in heaven watching over us. The role they played in my life was significant. I made a pledge that I would do something in my life that would touch others the way they touched so many during their stay on this earth. They are my angels.

I pray that you are watching over your beautiful granddaughter, Kallee. Each day I smile as I know you would enjoy every minute with her. We keep your memory alive with her each and every day.

Foreward

I STRUGGLED TO GET OUT OF BED TODAY. Heart was heavy. Eyes hurt. I struggled to open my puffy eyes and squinted as I watched the sun come up like a watermark behind the heavy clouds and fog. Then I heard it, the clap, clap of the rain on the roof. I made my way down to the coffee maker and was numb as I did the habitual task. But this wasn't a habitual day. I continued down the stairs and stepped outside to watch the rest of the sunrise and take in the morning mist. "He's crying," I thought, and my heavy heart spurred my own tears, the familiar swallow-trying to keep it all down and dam the flood of feelings that this day brought only two years ago.

I clenched my hands together and stared into the hazy sky . . . then I noticed a flicker of red. My head turned toward the slightly browned trees in our yard. Yes, the red beauty against the dismal backdrop. My cardinal . . . ah, both of my cardinals. They are here with me. The dam didn't hold. The warmth of the tear met my partial grin as I took a deep breath to take in the bit of comfort that I could muster to dull the pain.

You've probably had one of these days, or many. Why did they have to leave us? How can they not be here? Weren't they supposed to be here for this? They would have loved this place. Why does it feel like my heart has been ripped out of my chest? Longing to pick up the phone, hear their voices, hold their hands, and feel their arms around you . . . Loss — oh, the roller coaster of loss — If you've been on the ride, the one that you can't seem to get off, I hope you will read further and possibly relate to some of the rides, the journeys, within these pages and know that you are not alone.

CHAPTER ONE

Fighting for a Cure

THERE WE STOOD, surrounding her bed, holding her hand and stroking her hair and arms.

The look in her eyes was different today. I swallowed hard as I knew in my heart that she was ready. My father leaned over and said, "It's ok-we love you and always will." Within seconds Mom took her last breath.

Although my head was reminding me she was at peace and that the suffering was over, my heart was shattered. Over the last several months we watched our strong mother turn frail and weak. How could this be happening to her? She was one of the most amazing people I knew and not just because she was my mother. She was a devout Christian who treated everyone so kindly. She never drank or smoked and was so healthy. So how could this nasty disease invade her body?

Two years earlier our mother had begun losing weight for no reason, and we grew concerned. We went to numerous doctors until one amazing doctor finally found the cause: there was a tumor on our mother's kidney the size of a small football. This was removed and all was looking good, but then she started to lose weight again, and it turned out that it had metastasized to her lungs. There were spots throughout the lungs, so chemo and radiation were not options. The doctors suggested some experimental options, but it wasn't enough. . .

I have had loved ones go through this, but I was either ignorant or afraid to realize what a toll this takes on everyone involved. We were so thankful to all of the friends and family that reached out, sent cards, visited. I journaled my mom's battle, and I have found that it is really difficult to pick up and read. It's so hard to relive those emotions, the fear, the anxiety-but I will someday. It's a reminder, though, that each day, all over the world, there is someone sitting by a bedside, waiting for test results, praying and praying. Asking all of the same questions.

I feel that anyone who has lost a loved one to a disease that completely transforms a person's body and causes such suffering has to ask all of the same questions. Why? What else was there to do? What could I have done differently? Should we have gone somewhere else? For me, my only solace was to believe that God has His plan.

Once the cancer had gone into my mom's lungs, it progressed so quickly they had to put a tracheotomy in. I think the most difficult part of all was the inability to truly communicate during the last months. We talked a lot and her eyes told us so much, but I know there was so much more that she wanted to say. She was so weak that it was even difficult for her to write anything. We tried to lighten the mood every day and reminisced about funny memories, and her eyes would twinkle, but the pain kept getting greater and we saw her starting to fade.

Standing at the casket and looking at our beautiful mother, lying still, nearly floored me. The reality and finality kicked in. It's amazing how your legs really do buckle beneath you.

Several days after the funeral, as we were trying to pick up the pieces and comfort our father and each other, a good friend of ours who was so special to my mother asked us if we wanted to start a 5K Run/Walk in memory of our mother. What a special idea . . .

That year we started the Kalajainen Klassic 5K Run/Walk and have continued to hold it each year and raise money for the American Cancer Society. The event was such a great idea because my mother was a walker. She went to Prevention Walks all over the United States with her sister and was an active participant in the Race for a Cure each year. It is such a special day to honor our mother and so many others who have been impacted by this disease.

Many people direct their grief and energy toward trying to save others from the diseases that had taken their loved ones from them. Collectively they have raised millions of dollars, raised awareness and supported others who have been affected by these or similar diseases.

It is the love that they have in their hearts that gave them the courage and strength to do what they have done. Here are a few touching stories. . .

Lisa's Story:

I knew when I met Grant that he was the one. We hit it off right away. Grant Channell, a fair-skinned young man who was known for his sense of humor and sincere nature, grew up in the small town of Amanda, Ohio, with his parents and brother. He enjoyed playing sports with friends and life-guarding in the summers.

I met Grant when he moved to the Pittsburgh area to study at Robert Morris College, where he double-majored in finance and accounting. He loved life and brought so much happiness to my life. I wanted to be with him as much as possible and enjoyed every minute we were together, whether it was studying or hanging out with friends playing cards. . .

In 1989, the year of his graduation from college, his aunt noticed that the twenty-two-year-old had a peeling and flaking mole on his shoulder, and she urged him to have it evaluated by a physician. After a doctor's examination and tests, Grant was diagnosed with melanoma, the most serious type of skin cancer.

After that startling diagnosis, Grant underwent surgery and began a chemotherapy regimen of self-administered interferon, injecting the interferon into his leg each day. Initially, the chemotherapy made him extremely sick, but his condition eventually improved. He returned to work, and, after one year, his prognosis was good. All the while, Grant remained positive and committed to beating the cancer, and he continued to be monitored by his doctor through regular checkups.

He was doing so well and we were moving forward with our lives. We were married in 1992, and, a year later, a career opportunity for Grant took us away from Pittsburgh to Charleston, WV. Grant became the Director of Environmental Services for the Marriott Corporation at St. Francis Hospital. Shortly before we moved to West Virginia, Grant had his four-year checkup in the fall of 1993. The doctor found a swollen lymph node in Grant's neck, but told him not to worry. Like most people hoping for good news, we were more than relieved. We wanted so much for all to be well. The doctor instructed Grant to come back in one year.

Well, our entire lives changed before that next check-up.

In the early summer of 1994, Grant experienced a severe pain in his hip that he thought was a pulled muscle. The pain made it very agonizing for him to walk and to maintain his active lifestyle. While competing in a golf tournament, an activity he loved, Grant casually mentioned his hip pain and some of his medical history to a doctor who was golfing with him. This doctor was immediately very concerned about Grant and advised him to report to his doctor very soon, and Grant promised to do so. After the tournament, Grant and his team were presented with the first place trophy for their excellent play, but behind his grin of victory, Grant was in tremendous pain.

The severe pain soon took Grant to the emergency room. We found out that the melanoma had metastasized, spreading cancer to his bones and lymph nodes. The cancer had progressed beyond what Grant's doctor could treat. We were given a list of places to go for more advanced treatment, and we chose to go home to Pittsburgh for the expertise of world-renowned melanoma specialist John M. Kirkwood, M.D, at the University of Pittsburgh Cancer Institute (UPCI). We found Dr. Kirkwood's care very reassuring, and I know that it was the only time Grant felt comfortable with the care he received. Grant fought very hard and remained hopeful throughout the tests, treatments, sleepless nights, and horrible pain. He was always more concerned about me and how I was coping with the situation.

The last two months of Grant's life seemed like a nightmare, and, looking back, Grant's courage was unbelievable. Dr. Kirkwood communicated with other researchers worldwide about Grant's unusually virulent disease and Grant's tremendous fortitude. But, as this was happening, I had to watch the disease quickly change the man that I fell in love with. He lost weight and was very pale. No treatments were working, and the cancer seemed to appear in another area of his body each time another test was done. I stayed by his side night and day and was so thankful for the support of my family, especially my mom, friends and the hospital staff. During this time, Grant continued to work as many days as he could, always in constant pain. We made so many trips to the hospital for disease-related problems that it was difficult to keep a normal lifestyle.

During the last two weeks of his life, Grant was hospitalized. He could no longer sit up, stand, or

CHAPTER TWO

New Perspectives

Loss MADE ME EVALUATE EVERYTHING IN MY LIFE: what I stood for, how I wanted to live, the impact that I wanted to make on others' lives. I guess I was always pretty laid-back, although I was pretty intense when it came to work, schedules, pleasing everyone else-but now my philosophy is a bit different. It is what it is. You just don't have control all of the time and you have to appreciate every minute and every day. There are blessings all around us and it is important to 'be' in themoment and take time to appreciate and relish them. The sound of my daughter saying, "Good morning, Mommy, I love you"…my husband playing his guitar as a bedtime routine…stroking my daughter's hair as she peacefully sleeps…I could go on and on.

Sometimes it's easy though to get caught-up in the rat race and hurry through our days and moments to keep it all under control. I force myself to take a breath and re-balance to make sure my focus is on my family and my passions just as my parents encouraged me to do. After all of these years, I still have this instinct to pick up the phone and call them when I need advice or loving support.

Although losing loved ones to death has been the most difficult loss that I have experienced, loss comes in many forms. Losing a job (yep), divorce (yep), miscarriage (yep), and so many other types of loss often take you through the same stages of grief, but they truly do make you stronger, more empathetic maybe. These experiences have made me much more aware and appreciative of all that God has blessed me with.

None of us really knows how a death or a major life-changing event is going to affect us. A common reaction is to take a step back and reevaluate priorities. The things that once seemed so important take on a different meaning, and typically the people and moments that might have been taken for granted in our lives become all the more precious.

A story in *O Magazine* hit home with me: Patricia Kline from Menlo Park, California, was inspired to transition from marketing executive to baker. Her mother suffered from Alzheimer's disease and was hospitalized after a fall. To deal with stress and anguish, Patricia resorted to baking pies, a ritual she shared with her mom when she was a child.

Kline mentioned that she was struck by how tiny her mother's world had become and started baking small items and named them "ipies." She stated that, when her mother could no longer speak, she felt that telling her mother about her baking calmed her. They were still communicating through the language of baking.

Patricia's mother passed away, and the economy forced her and her husband to downsize. Although she was inclined to return to her high-paying career avenue, she resisted.

"When you lose so much, you discover that your identity isn't made up of material things, it's about what you can do with your brain and enthusiasm. Now was the time to take a chance and do something with passion," expressed Kline.

Her efforts paid off, and she won a coveted space at her local farm's market, living her dream. I get inspired just going to her website and seeing her smiling face.

O Magazine, November 2010, shared Patricia Kline's story. To learn more about "ipies" and Patricia's story, go to **http://www.theipiestore.com/**

When I am having a difficult day or I have things out of perspective, I think of the following individuals who have shared their journeys. A smiling face can hide the burdens that one has endured. It strengthens me to know such strong and faithful individuals who muster the will to remain positive despite their losses. It's amazing how people reach inside themselves to find the strength to go on and gain a new perspective on life.

Linda's Story:

Every time I look at my beautiful granddaughter, I thank God that He gave me the strength to go on. I am constantly reminded of how fortunate I am to have her in my life. Raising a child in my fifties is not what I had expected, but she has been my angel, and she probably takes care of me as much as I take care of her. Loss, despite how difficult it is, gives you a different perspective on life. Priorities change, and we learn to be thankful for every day we have with our loved ones.

The nights were long in the hospital as my 2½-year-old daughter, Brenda, was fighting for her life. She was diagnosed with neuroblastoma (cancer of the nervous system). I was only 20 years old, and I just couldn't believe that this was happening. After we lost her, I went into silence. I had an 8-month-old son, and it took me a while to realize that, in my depression, I had shut him out. I felt like I couldn't even deal with him. I had to take a hard look at myself and realize that I couldn't be selfish and had to be thankful for the son that I had left. It took a while, but I then refocused my energies on being the best mother that I could be to my son. I had to redirect my thoughts and emotions to him. We became very close, and then I was fortunate enough to have another daughter when he was five. My daughter Lori was a joy as well.

They were both young and vibrant children, eager to please and good-natured. Then one evening my son asked me if he could ride his motorbike with his friends on the railroad tracks. I told him no, as I always did. But this night he begged and begged. I finally gave in.

It was getting dark and he still wasn't home. We got in touch with one of his friends to see where he was. The friend said my son had gone home to get something, but he never came back to meet them. His friend said he figured my son had just stayed at home.

I had a sinking feeling in my stomach. My husband went searching for him. They found him, and it was too late. He had decided to take a different path to meet his friends, a path with a cable strung across the road that he wasn't aware of.

How could God take two of my children away from me?? I can't handle this. What did I do to deserve this? It was fourteen years after I had lost my infant daughter.

Once again I fell into depression and found myself ignoring my daughter. All I wanted was to have David back. There I was again, angry at what had been taken away from me instead of thankful for God blessing me with my daughter Lori.

She did need me, and I am thankful that I found a way to snap out of my funk and work through my grief in a healthier way. Lori was having a difficult time with his death as well. She wrote a letter as her way of saying goodbye. I've cherished this letter and am amazed that she found her own way to grieve and deal with this tragedy as an eleven-year-old.

To You

Thinking about you makes my heart ache.

Remembering the times we shared together,

Knowing that you are gone forever,

I feel so guilty.

Expressing my feelings was hard to do.

I really couldn't say that I loved you.

I wish I would have said those three little words.

I try to remember only the good times and forget all the bad,

but popping up in my mind are those times of tension when

those three little words "I hate you" were spoken.

Fighting with you was never much fun, because I was the

youngest one.

Praying to God, "Please bring him back!"

I know that that is not possible, for you are gone. Accepting

this was the hardest thing I ever had to do, but someday DAVEY,

I'll be with you. I LOVE YOU!!

Looking back, though, I think David's death impacted her more than I realized. In the midst of all of this, I went through a divorce as well. Two male influences were removed from Lori's life.

Lori was searching. She had her own struggles. As she got older, she moved to Kansas along with my infant granddaughter, Kirstie. Although I always supported her, it was so difficult to have her so far away Then one day, I got the call I had secretly wanted. She told me she was coming home. Lori and Kirstie moved back home. It was great to have them around again, and Lori was busy working two jobs, raising her daughter, and being a strong single mom. We became inseparable again. I saw her finding her own way and was so proud.

I was watching Kirstie one evening, and we had run to the store. When we got home, there was a note from Lori. She had stopped by to pick up Kirstie.

Kirstie and I decided to wait for her to return. Then the phone rang. I still get weak in my knees as I think about the sound of his voice. It was . . .

"There's been an accident . . . it's Lori. She went off the road. . . She didn't make it."

It was fourteen years after I had lost David - the same number of years that were between losing my youngest and David. I just thought, there is no way that I can handle this. Stunned and in disbelief, I looked over at four-year-old Kirstie. I knew at that moment that I had to be strong for her. I'm all she has.

I decided not to take Kirstie to the funeral. I felt that she was too young and would not understand. How could she understand when I couldn't explain "why" this happened?

Kirstie went through many changes. She would become very angry and was so frustrated (always taking it out on me). All along, I knew she loved and needed me but was just too young to accept or understand the loss she had to deal with.

I had never really got involved with support groups as I was dealing with the loss of my other children. I found it difficult to reach out to others. I kept so much of my feelings and grief tucked inside. Now I wasn't alone in my grief.

So, a few years after Lori passed away, I heard about a support group for children at the local church called the "Touch of Love." I decided that Kirstie and I would attend. This was best decision that I made.

During this time, Kirstie and I began to heal together. She had the opportunity to talk with other children who had lost a parent. We both found that we needed to talk about her death and our feelings. At the last session of the series of workshops, Kirstie shared a poem that she wrote about her mother. This was Kirstie's closure, and I was so proud of her.

She, like her mother, found a way to say goodbye in the written word. She looks so much like her mother, and I was so proud and thankful that I had her to help me carry on Lori's memory. She brightens my life every day. She is a strong, talented and social little girl. Once again, despite what was taken away from me, I have to thank God for what I have.

It's difficult being a grandmother raising a grandchild, but I was fortunate to get involved in an organization called "Grandparents Raising Grandchildren." I couldn't believe how many people are in the same shoes. This group is for grandparents and others raising children. We meet once a month. It is so comforting to have a place to share your feelings and problems with others that are in similar situations. Last fall, our group and others from across the state of Pennsylvania went to Jumonville for a retreat. We all had similar needs, and it was a most peaceful and rewarding experience. I think all of the grandparents had a special connection with their grandchildren that will never be forgotten.

Most people do not know my story because I'm a very private person, but it helps to share my story with the Grandparents Raising Children group. I realize that you don't have to be silent and that sometimes your own struggles can help someone else.

My goal in life now is to be the best mother / grandmother to Kirstie that I can be-giving her all the love and guidance that I can. I know at this stage of my life I have to be in good physical condition and pray for good health in order to do so. There is a purpose for all of the hardships that I have had to endure in my life.

I am proud to say that Kirstie just graduated from high school and started college, a beautiful young lady, and that, despite my losses, I am so fortunate to have her.

Although I was ready for a new life, this added a whole new dimension. I had never had to go through anything like this before, and it was difficult to grasp the impact-I'm still having a difficult time. Then, shortly after losing Andy, my grandmother, stricken with cancer, lost her battle. This was also bittersweet as we knew she wasn't going to pull through this and we couldn't stand to see her suffer. My grandfather, a doctor, was taking full-time care of the love of his life, and it was sadly affecting his health as well.

When Grandma passed our family pulled together, and a lot of the bitterness and anxiety that was filling our lives, with the pending divorce as well as seeing her struggle with her life, seemed to subside as the reality of losing people really put things into perspective. The things that used to seem so important just didn't matter anymore-especially the material things.

My Mercedes broke down on my way to my grandmother's funeral, and I completely missed her burial. My son had been chosen to be a pallbearer, and I was now going to miss out on that honor as well. I was so upset, and I just wondered how much more God was going to put on my plate.

After the funeral, my grandfather told me not to worry as he would sell me my grandmother's car at a very affordable price instead of having me put money into this car. Finally, a stroke of good luck. Several days later, my daughter lost my set of car keys returning home from the mailbox. I attempted to call Grandpa all day to see if he had a spare set. Numerous unanswered phone calls throughout the morning and early afternoon gave us a sense that something just wasn't right. Initially my mom and I both assumed he was at the gym and/or visiting friends. Mom decided to go check on him, and I asked her to call me when she got there to let me know Grandpa was fine. Well, the call came, but imagine the shock when I heard Mom say, "My dad is dead." Of course, the shock and panic hit me again. Later I asked a friend how the kids had reacted when I was shrieking in disbelief. She told me they had blank stares on their faces and my son had said, "What? ANOTHER death?"

We were all just devastated. All in a matter of two months we had lost three people in our lives — barely enough time to catch our breaths. I am still trying to be so strong for my children and help them to make sense of it all when I don't even know that I can make sense of it. Usually I break down in the mornings when they are still sleeping. But what I find interesting is the strength that they give me.

My son has been so insightful and has taken on this grown-up role at only eleven. At his father's funeral he went up to every person in line at the viewing, introducing himself and saying, "Hi, I'm Andrew; I'm Andy's son." An act of courage that I'm not sure most adults could perform. He was even seen going to get tissues for some of the people in line grieving. At my grandfather's memorial luncheon I started crying, and he walked over, put his arm around me, and said, "It's OK, Mom. It was like God was giving Grandpa the best Christmas gift ever. He took him home to be with his wife who he loved so much." At that point I realized the true blessings in my life: my children, my family.

We have all started to attend grieving sessions at the Caring Place and, although our situation is tough, hearing others' stories puts things into perspective for us It could always be worse. I think of all of the good times that we got to share with all of our loved ones, and, although going through the divorce prior to Andy's death was very difficult for all of us, the kids got to do things with him that they probably wouldn't have done when we were still a joint unit. They went to Disney World, Camelback Mountain, Mt. Gretna and had many more fun trips and some wonderful memories with him. Right before Andy's death he had started photo books for each of them, with pictures from their trip to Disney World. He had them all finished except for the captions. His sis-

ter-in-law put the finishing touches on each of the albums and wrapped them up as a gift from their daddy. How touching that they were able to get a Christmas gift from him!

We all have a new perspective on life. My husband went to bed that October night and never woke up. Some say he truly died of a broken heart: it was enlarged, and a dysrhythmia proved fatal.. He had a future planned; he had his Halloween costume on his dresser; he had plans with the kids . . . he didn't expect it all to end.

The simple things are the most important, and time with your loved ones is most important. It's not the car you drive, the trips you take, the clothes you wear that make you important. It's what you do with your life, how you treat others, and learning to speak from your heart. . .

I think of all of the things that Andy and I were haggling over in the divorce, over who would get what -and now all of those "things" that he got are just gathering dust. I don't want things to gather dust in my life ever again.. I want to live each blessed moment with my kids and a new special person in my life to the fullest and never lose sight of the fact that we are not in charge and our time here is short. For years, I've always reminded my children each day to thank God for something. I don't care if it's that the sun is shining or that they woke up healthy, but it's important to be grateful for each day we're given. This now has more meaning than ever to our family.

DARKEST MOMENTS:

Breaking down at the oddest times, such as when sitting at a Parent/Teacher meeting for our daughter and realizing that I am the ONLY parent now; having dinner at Hollywood Casino and remembering our love of gambling; or seeing the times in my son's life as he grows older when I will have to play the part of the father, and don't know anything about it. He put on a tie Christmas morning and I couldn't tie it for him-his dad would always do that. Sadly, I don't have my "sounding board" for what is right for our children. I pray that he guides me from heaven, because our love for our kids was one thing we both agreed upon.

BRIGHTEST MOMENTS:

The brightest moments are when I see my children doing things that would make their father proud or the way they are kind and caring to others. What I went through at forty is way different from how children at nine and eleven experience all of this. I know God has great plans in store for them and I'm so proud of the strength they've exhibited. My son has maintained a 96% GPA for all 3 marking periods this year, and my daughter has nurtured and taken care of several new friendships. They exhibit love, strength and patience when others could have turned to depression, anger and darkness. My children have their father on a pedestal, and it's my goal in life to keep him on that pedestal in their minds. My children have taught me so much in these past few months. I'm blessed to have them in my life.

————— • —————

I have known Nicole Devitt as a young college graduate through today and feel blessed to have such a bright star in my universe. This gal is the most optimistic person that I have encountered in my lifetime. The past 12 months have been extremely challenging for her and her family, especially her children with the loss of their Dad and maternal grandparents. The divorce process challenging in itself, when it involves small children had its intense moments, but somehow this buoyant creature of life and light has managed to rise above the ugliness and provide a stable environment for herself and her beautiful children. She will instill in them a great zest for life and provide an amazing sense of strength and security for AJ and Carson. Although the atmosphere between her and Andy was not at its best when he passed, the most important job ever in her life will be raising strong and independent children.

The Hoffmans, The Devitts & Andy will be proud of her most important role!

— **Rosemarie Zdrojewski**

I am drowning in tears. Strengthen me as you promised.

Psalm 119:28 *(GOD'S WORD)*

CHAPTER THREE
Keeping Their Memory Alive

THE LITTLE ANGEL IN MY BRIEF CASE, the Bicentennial quarters, the oversized flannel, medals, pictures . . . I could go on and on. Guess I am pretty sentimental, but mementos of my loved ones are so precious to me. I love to show my daughter items that belonged to her grandparents and what those meant to them.

My dad was obsessed with collecting Bicentennial quarters, and to this day I get this warm feeling when I get one in change and just smile and look up into the sky. My mom loved angels and books. I can't tell you how many times I have reached into my briefcase and held this little angel of hers just to give me some strength.

We always have a toast to loved ones on birthdays, anniversaries of their deaths, holidays. I had made CDs for my sisters of songs that reminded us of our parents, and playing those songs provides such comfort and really does keep their memory alive for me.

Often, life's pressures cloud our feelings, and it can be tempting to numb ourselves in order to get through the day, but many professionals encourage us to find ways to memorialize our lost loved ones. Tokens, rituals, pictures or clothing that remind us of our loved ones can provide strength and help us to move on with our lives.

I found that the battle between holding on and letting go can be very taxing, and we have to remember that having these mixed feelings is very natural and part of the journey. I know that I often watch the DVD that we made of my father for his funeral when I am missing him or read one of my mother's favorite scriptures when I want to feel close to her. My sister, on the other hand, has not been able to watch the DVD as it is just too difficult for her, but she has one of her bedrooms set up the exact way my father had his bedroom before he passed away, and that environment is very comforting to her. It is a very personal thing, and only you will know what works for you.

Some of the passages I have included throughout this book come from one of my mother's books, Promises from God's Word. She had underlined the passages in it that meant something to her. She lost her mother when she was a teenager, and at that time, she said, no one talked about death or grief, there were no support groups. One day her mother was there and then she wasn't, and life had to go on. Each time I read the various passages I regret that I didn't inquire more about her mother and her "feelings." We were very close, but my mother's generation wasn't encouraged to share emotions and feelings as we are today. I wish I had been more empathetic to how difficult it must have been for her. Just as I am sad

Weeping may last for the night,
but there is a song of joy in the morning.

Psalm 30:5b *(GOD'S WORD)*

CHAPTER FOUR

Celebrating Their Lives

Aᴛ ᴍᴏsᴛ ꜰᴜɴᴇʀᴀʟs, you will hear reminiscing about the decedents, how they lived their lives, and their passions. These passions signify so much about who those persons were and the impact they have had on others.

One of my father's passions was golf. For years we held a golf outing called the Kalajainen Klassic, and when my father passed away in October, my sisters and I carried on with the golf outing in memory of our father and some others whom we have lost. It is a time for family and friends who love the game of golf to get together and enjoy the fellowship and the game, while raising money for the American Heart Association. We dedicate the day to Captain Don and celebrate his life and the ways he enriched all our lives. My dad taught me how to play golf when I was eleven, and I will be eternally grateful for that and the memories of being with him on the golf course.

My father also loved woodworking and making boxes. Although I never inherited his innate talent for woodworking, I have set out to make custom memory boxes out of wood. I have at least four boxes that he had made for me, and they are precious. I hope that the memory boxes that I make will not only give me the opportunity to carry on my father's passion but wrap-up and store precious memories for others.

My mother loved angels, and my sisters and I each split up the numerous angels in our mom's collection. I have some in my daughter's room. I love talking to her about angels and she has grown to love them as well. She never had a chance to meet her grandparents, but I see my dad's sense of humor in her, and I want to cultivate their passions in her so she has a way to connect with them somehow. At my baby shower, my sister gave me a framed picture of our parents, with the following inscription:

To our precious baby
From heaven up above
We'll be your guardian angels
And watch over you with love.

Grandma and Grandpa
Kalajainen

Each night as we say our prayers, we pray for Grandma and Grandpa Kalajainen in Heaven.

Celebrating the lives of our lost loved ones and carrying on their passions can be comforting and healing. Personally, it has helped me to reflect on the person that I want to be as well as what I want others to remember about me. When you carry on the positive influence of your loved ones, it can extend through the generations.

Shirley's Story:

— • —

My childhood was joyful and carefree, having parents who loved me and provided a secure home for me. That serenity was shattered, at least for a time, the day my mom suddenly died. I was fourteen years old and was very close to my mom. She had had surgery for a ruptured appendix and suffered a fatal blood clot to the lung.

My mom was in the hospital from Friday until Tuesday, when she died. In those days it was the hospital's policy to not allow children under the age of sixteen to visit patients. As a result, my six-year-old brother and I never got to see her once she was taken to the hospital. That was very hard to deal with and made me angry for some time.

The pain of loss was so intense, I didn't want to go on without her. I remember at the gravesite thinking, "I will just jump in and go with her."

Life continued on, however, and the pain continued as well. The family was all hurting, and we couldn't talk about Mom and how we felt because of the agonizing pain. We would just begin to cry and then drop the conversation.

Within a year after my mom's death the last of my three older siblings moved out, and I became the homemaker, caring for my seven-year-old brother and my dad, who worked three jobs. As a result, my brother and I spent many hours at home alone. We did not have TV or telephone, so life was very lonely. It was especially difficult coming home after school to an empty house, where we previously would come home to sweet aromas in the kitchen and my mom's welcoming voice. We had a dear neighbor lady who would often have us in for supper when Dad was working the afternoon shift. We were thankful for her kindness.

The fact that I had others to care for helped me to go on and try to have as happy a home as possible for those of us who remained. We also had a very loving, supportive church family who cared about us.

It took several years to work through the loss and have the courage to speak of the pain, anger, frustration, sadness and loneliness. It seemed that in the early 1950s there were not that many resources available to those going through loss. Some twenty years after the loss of my mother, I met a woman who was a counselor by profession. We became good friends, and she was a great help to me in working through all the "stuff" that goes along with loss. I am grateful God brought her into my life.

My four siblings and I remain close and recognize the value of relationships in life. We are grateful we had our mom as long as we did and for all of the things that she taught us. Her favorite scripture was Psalm 119:165, "Great peace have they which love thy law and nothing shall offend them." She was a very peaceful, positive, loving, cheerful person, and her memory will always be with us. Knowing we will someday be reunited with her in heaven is a great comfort to us.

A few years after losing my mom, I met and married my wonderful, sensitive husband. He has helped me work through the pain of loss.

Our life was good; we had three married daughters and six beautiful grandchildren, and we were a happy family. My husband had taken early retirement, and we were thoroughly enjoying the freedom that gave us. It gave us time to help remodel our daughter Jeanne's house to prepare a nursery for their first child. Little did we know how much we would value the time we had spent with our daughter during this venture.

After just four short years, we received the news that Jeanne had colon cancer. It was devastating

Let your mercy comfort me as you promised.

Psalm 119:76 *(GOD'S WORD)*

CHAPTER FIVE
Comforting Signs

Each morning I look out my window to find my two cardinals. Usually within a few minutes, I see them in one of our trees. Their red feathers blazon against the green of the trees or the white snow. This couple of cardinals has been here since I moved in and have become a symbol of my parents to me. Even my daughter gets excited when she sees them and yells "I see your cardinals Mommy!"

My parents loved to watch the birds, and now it's my way of finding the comfort of their presence in this life without them. It makes me smile when I see them out there and hear their song. Some may think it is a little crazy, but the more I spoke with others who have suffered loss, the more I discovered that they too had found their own signs that were comforting to them.

One of the most bittersweet tasks that usually have to be done following the loss of a loved one is to go through their things, clean-out their house, keep or discard. I still tear up when I think about going through my parents' house. My dad built our house and we lived in the same house our entire life. Needless to say, when you don't move, the purging that would typically occur didn't. Although this was very difficult, I also found it comforting and cleansing. The house was full of 50+ years of memories, laughter and tears. My sisters and I spent days and days doing this but it gave us time to reminisce, remember and just feel their presence.

Many peculiar things happened while we going through the process though. Light bulbs popped for no reason, a strange message on an answering machine when the phone had already been turned off, the mercury light that had been burned out for many years (so tall that you needed a bucket truck to change it) suddenly came one on night, and so on. I can't explain them but nonetheless, they were oddly comforting to all of us.

At first we were uncomfortable mentioning this to anyone but we have encountered so many people that have experienced similar occurrences and that is why I share this. A pragmatic person, of Christian faith, reared to believe that these could be nothing more than coincidences — I just gave in and was open to the comforting side of them. Everyone's situations are different but once again it's about finding what comforts you and being open to whatever this could be. Here are some comforting signs that have been shared.

———————— • ————————

Blackbird, Blackbird

When my father passed away, we were sitting in his back yard and this black bird flew into the tree next to us. He began his "cawing," almost like he was trying to say something. So many times since I have lost my father, this black bird will show up when I am thinking of him the most, "cawing" to me. I laugh and smile and find comfort that he is watching over me.

— **Lauri Kalajainen**

Angel in the Sky

My grandmother died shortly after I got married. It always made me so sad to know she would never meet my children and that they would never know her. After my first daughter was born, I talked to her about her great-grandmother a lot, how I knew Gram would've loved her. One day, when Courtney was about a year old, I was "spider-swinging" with her at the playground, singing to her, and talking about Gram. It was getting late in the day, and the sky was gorgeous, with pinks and oranges, and fluffy clouds. I got a little teary talking about Gram, but looked out at the sky and noticed a cloud perfectly shaped like an angel. It was beautiful. The outline was all white and the round face had a pink glow. I was amazed!

CHAPTER SIX
Hidden Heroes

EVERY DAY PEOPLE GIVE OF THEMSELVES, from the heart. They have altered their life's missions or are doing things that touch others' lives. They have been inspired to reach out to others and make a difference following some type of a loss or change in their lives. Often they go unnoticed, but they ask for nothing in return because they feel their lives are enriched by what they do and that is inspiration in itself.

Several years ago I had the opportunity to be part of a new team in a larger organization that was to head up a new initiative within the company. We were all excited about this venture and grew to be a close knit team. One of the team members, Patrick, ended up impacting our lives in ways we would have never imagined. Being in the corporate world was a change from his life as a flight nurse/EMT but Patrick embraced this change and went back to get his Master's Degree, got braces, became a volunteer at the newly launched Highmark Caring Place for Grieving Children and became an avid biker and runner. He also volunteered as a paramedic, participated in numerous fund raisers and was a baseball and softball coach. He inspired us all.

We became friends with Patrick's beautiful wife Liz and their children. Their middle child, Amanda, had the most serious form of epilepsy and a smile that would light-up a room. Patrick and Liz cared for her so unconditionally and never complained of the level of care that she required and the complex medical problems that were a challenge for them every day.

In November of 2001, they lost beautiful Amanda at 14. It was devastating. Patrick and his family attended sessions at Highmark Caring Place, where Patrick was already a volunteer, for grief support for them and their surviving children.

Patrick and Liz tried to turn their grief into something positive and focused on the lives that were saved by the donation of Amanda's organs and they set-up several memorials and projects in Amanda's memory.

Two years later, on a terrible rainy night, I had this horrible feeling that something was wrong. The next morning I received a call from one of my previous co-workers and she told me that Patrick was killed in a car accident the night before. I just shook. All I could think of was that Amanda needed her Daddy.

Their daughter Ashley was also in the car but thank goodness she survived and was going to be OK. My heart went out to Liz and the kids. Not only did they lose an amazing father, we all lost a wonderful friend and the world lost a special person.

Patrick's impact lives on through many of us and he was posthumously honored as a Highmark Blue Cross Blue Shield "Volunteer of the Year". He touched many lives in his short 42 years on this earth.

Liz went on to start a company dedicated to Amanda called *Panda and Associates, LLC*. Amanda's nickname was Amanda Panda. Liz shares this quote on her website:

"I learned that you can get beyond grief. Although it will always be a part of you, I learned that you can derive lessons from negative experiences…To heal yourself, you have to give to others. That is your responsibility."

Gianas, G. "Nurses who served in Vietnam: Silent heroes."
Journal of Emergency Nursing, Vol.20. No 3, 247-249.

I later became a volunteer at the Highmark Caring Place and understood why Patrick was such a dedicated volunteer. It is an amazing organization full of hidden heroes helping children and their families deal and cope with their grief. The Caring Place fosters openness and sharing of the various emotions that accompany grief demystifying it for children allowing them to express their feelings in a safe environment.

As an adult losing my parents and other loved ones, I still felt unequipped to effectively deal with my grief and I feel it is so important that resources like this exist for families. You don't have to go through loss alone.

Although I didn't attend any grief support groups myself, I felt God provided this support group around me. Daily, people come in and out of our lives and I believe that God does place certain people in your life for a reason. It's interesting how lives intertwine and at some level we all have commonalities.

The other day I was having a casual conversation with someone I had gotten to know over the years through work. She is one of those people that is positive and just makes everyone feel good when you speak with her. I asked how her daughter was doing and she proceeded to fill me in and tells me her daughter is getting married. She is telling me about her son-in-law and just happens to mention that he started an organization called *Uplifting Athletes* in memory of his father to raise funds for rare cancer. She didn't realize that I was writing this book. I knew God meant for her to mention this and immediately I wanted to hear more about his story.

I came to learn that Scott's father passed away of kidney cancer, same as my mom. He and his family shared the same frustrations that we did that there just wasn't that much treatment available for this type of cancer. Scott just didn't stop with being frustrated though, he took action.

Stronger Every Day ~ Scott's Story:

————————— • —————————

In the fall of 2002, I was a wide receiver on the Penn State football team. I was on my way home from practice one day when my cell phone rang. When I saw my mom's name on the screen, my heart dropped to my stomach. It was one of those calls that I knew was going to bring bad news. Sure enough, I answered the phone and she was so choked up that she couldn't even talk. I pulled into the parking lot in front of the Nittany Lion Inn while she composed herself enough to tell me that my father had been diagnosed with renal cell carcinoma (commonly known as kidney cancer). They were told that he'd be lucky to see me graduate just six months later.

Joe Paterno often told us, "You're never as good as you think you are when you win, and you're never as bad as you think you are when you lose."Lessons like this helped me to develop a pretty level head when times get tough. You hear about people beating cancer all the time, right? My dad had lived a healthy lifestyle - he didn't drink or smoke and remained active as a high school baseball coach for 30-plus years. He was a fighter. He was going to be a survivor. Everything was going to be OK.

That fall, I went with my parents to the best medical centers in the mid-Atlantic region. Everywhere we went, though, we were told that nothing could be done. In my mind, that meant we just hadn't found the right doctor yet. We finally got a referral to Johns Hopkins, which in my mind was like going to see the Wizard of Oz. As excited as I was to go, I was equally heartbroken when we left. The doctor didn't even stay in the room long enough to close the door. All he said was that there was nothing they could do; he suggested that we simply go home and enjoy the time we had left.

On the way back to State College, it hit me that there had to be more to this story. So I called the American Cancer Society and they explained to me that each cancer is a different disease with unique molecular pathologies and treatment protocols. Since kidney cancer does not typically respond to standard first-line treatments, such as chemotherapy or radiation, it was not one of the organization's priorities.

They were sorry, and I was now more desperate. My next call was to the Kidney Cancer Association.

That is when I learned why nothing could be done: Kidney cancer affected fewer than 200,000 Americans and was classified as a "rare disease," meaning there was little financial incentive to make and market new treatments.

So now what? By the time I walked into my apartment, I was pretty aggravated. My roommate and teammate, Damone Jones, greeted me as usual. Except this time, when he asked how my day was, I expressed my frustration with the situation that my family was facing. It wasn't that "nothing could be done." It was that it wasn't important enough to do anything. Without hesitation, Damone shrugged his shoulders and suggested that we do something. "We're Penn State football players," he said. "If we do something stupid, it's on the front page of the papers. Let's take advantage of the position that we're in and use that spotlight to make a difference."

Damone and I started brainstorming in the locker room, and the team rallied around the idea of taking our summer lifting competition, opening it up to the public and using it as an opportunity to raise some money and tell our story about kidney cancer as a rare disease. So we talked with the coaches and approached administrators. They encouraged us to run with it.

At the same time, my family had been referred by the Kidney Cancer Association to a specialist at UPMC. The doctor suggested surgery, and we did not hesitate. It was a complicated procedure, as the tumor touched five vital organs and was starting to encroach on my father's vena cava. Surgeons had to remove two ribs and go through the diaphragm just to access it. A second procedure removed half of his left lung because the cancer had metastasized before it was found. My family spent Easter together in the hospital. While I was there, teammate Dave Costlow called to see how things were going. He had heard about what Damone and I were trying to organize and offered to help.

So Damone, Dave and I approached Deloris Brobeck, our football team's academic services assistant. She knew we were up to something when we walked into her office with smiles from ear to ear. She welcomed our idea to hold a weightlifting fundraiser with open arms as any good "team mom" would and helped us to start organizing. As word spread around the locker room, our teammates rallied around the idea. This was turning into something special almost overnight.

Back home, my dad was recovering as expected. He was jogging before he was supposed to be able to walk. He even beat the odds and was there to watch me graduate with my Engineering degree that spring.

The first annual Lift For Life took place in July 2003. About half of our team voluntarily signed up for one of strength coach John Thomas' toughest workouts imaginable. A handful of friends, family members and fans showed up to make their donations and show their support. The media enjoyed this rare opportunity to cover Penn State football in the middle of the summer. Our efforts raised more than $10,000 for the Kidney Cancer Association. But more than anything, we were excited about the potential that this had in every respect.

The following year Lift For Life raised another $40,000. One evening after this second annual event, Dave Costlow and I were writing thank-you notes with the help of another volunteer, Carrie Konosky. It was getting late, and we were laughing about the fact that in just two years we had raised more than $50,000 for the Kidney Cancer Association (KCA) but had never actually met anyone from the organization. We discussed going to visit their office in Chicago, but the only weekend that we were all available started the next day. I called the KCA and asked if they would be around that weekend. They said they would, but were also holding their biggest patient conference of the year. We thought this would be a perfect time to visit, but their small staff was nervous that the timing of our visit would not allow us to spend quality time together. We decided this was a risk worth taking.

Last-minute airfare from State College to Chicago was not an option. But it turned out that a rental car was. We took a big old Buick from the rental lot back to our apartments and hit the road around midnight. Mapquest said it was only a 10-hour drive. About an hour outside of Chicago, the KCA called to see if we were still coming. Fresh off a rest-stop nap in Indiana, we explained that our ETA was around noon. They said our timing was perfect because the keynote speaker scheduled for lunch was no longer able to make it. I was asked to fill in. When we pulled up to the curb, the valet took our car, and the three of us were ushered right up to the stage. The irony was that we still had not met anyone from the KCA yet.

The next five or 10 minutes were among the best of my life. We shared our story and were interrupted three times by standing ovations. The audience lived in the same world that I did - a world in which people tell them as a statement of fact that nothing can be done. Well guess what? We are Penn State and we are doing something. The medical advisory board was moved to tears. They dedicated their careers to a disease that was respected by few. They were no longer alone.

This weekend proved to be a truly life changing experience for me. I realized that if nothing else, our actions had the ability to inspire people with courage, spirit and hope. Our effort was always bigger than me and my father, but this was the first time that I experienced just how big it was. I felt a sense of obligation to help it reach its full potential. The drive back to Pennsylvania gave us plenty of time to think and talk about the future.

I had exhausted my football eligibility and enjoyed my last semester as a "normal" college student. The weekend of a home game, I met Dave Wozniak, one of our loyal donors for the first time and offered to give his family a tour of the football facilities. He shared some of his professional experiences in advertising and branding with me and selflessly offered to help. We communicated on a regular basis the rest of the semester and shared a vision for how big this could become.

My dad watched me graduate - this time with a master's degree - in December 2004. I transitioned the leadership of our student organization to members of the next class on the football team, and I moved to Washington, D.C., to work as an engineer at Clark Construction Company.

As college kids, it's pretty easy to dream. Making dreams a reality takes some serious planning, though. And that's where Wozniak excelled. We discussed the fact that kidney cancer was one of nearly 7,000 rare diseases and that all 30 million rare disease patients face similar challenges living in a world of isolation. The idea of creating an organization that could effectively use college football as a platform to make rare diseases a national priority seemed daunting. But the potential impact was even more exciting.

In the midst of all this, my father's cancer came back with a vengeance later that summer. It was difficult for me because I had just started my dream job and was trying to continue to grow our efforts to fund kidney cancer research, but we were running out of time. There were literally not enough hours in the day. The cancer eventually took my father, but it never beat him. What we learned from his fight inspired a movement that will change the world for people in similar situations.

All 30 million of them.

I had always said that this was bigger than him. When he passed away on October 17, 2005, that became the new reality for everyone else who had joined us in our fight.

Over the course of the next year, Dave Wozniak and I spent most of our free time working together, researching, writing and editing a business plan that would evolve our organization and see us through the critical next steps. It had to be a coordinated effort. Through this, Uplifting Athletes was born with the mission of aligning college football with rare diseases and raising them as a national priority.

After the Penn State chapter's Lift For Life that year, I got an e-mail from Carol Willie in Oregon. She thanked me for bringing attention to kidney cancer, because both her husband and her father were kidney cancer patients. She said that she and her husband had taken their kids, 12-year-old Alison and 7-year-old Eric, cross-country to lobby on Capitol Hill and they were surprised by what they learned. One of the staffers they met was shocked that the newest drug was not being covered by insurance … until they told him it was for kidney cancer. The staffer quickly explained that it was not a "popular cancer." Eric offered the staffer a colored bracelet (for kidney cancer) before they left, but the staffer politely declined, stating that they could not accept gifts.

knew I had to do: I was going to keep J.R. safe, and we were going to battle this disease together. This vibrant, independent man needed me, and I was about to take on the biggest challenge of my life.

Over the next five years, we were inseparable. I would spend days and nights by his side. There were many hospital stays involving blood and platelet transfusions. He had two stem-cell transplants and many life-threatening infections. Additional surgeries, such as those to extract his teeth and open his sinus passages, were necessary due to complications brought on by the multiple myeloma. Because of his weakened condition, J.R was prone to having adverse reactions to even the simplest illness. A cold for J.R. could ultimately result in a hospital stay. I lived day-to-day in fear of what was going to happen next. All of this became a regular way of life for us.

With God's grace and the best team of specialists, J.R. always managed to pull through. Our doctors and hospital staff became close friends. J.R. would continue to amaze everyone with his "nine lives"! The sound of my voice is what J.R. put his trust in. There were many times during his illness when he couldn't understand what was happening. With so many complications, in many ways I was relieved he was unaware of how extremely ill he was. I lived those days out mostly numb.

The last three weeks of J.R.'s life were spent in intensive care on a respirator. Since he had beaten the odds against him so many times, I hoped and prayed this would be another setback he would pull through. Even though family and friends came every day to show their love for both of us, I felt so alone. I was beginning to feel very scared and helpless. Everything was being done for him that the doctors could do. The prognosis, as days went on, didn't look good. I kept believing we'd get another miracle, but this time too many things had gone wrong. J.R. was losing his battle to live. We had fought this life-threatening disease together for five years, and I didn't want to believe I would not be taking J.R. home with me this time. J.R.'s courageous battle ended December 28, 2000. He was surrounded by all the family and friends he loved who loved him in return.

J.R. did give me a gift the day he died. Those twinkling, turquoise blue eyes opened for me. I saw again the handsome, boyish man I loved more than my own life. He could not speak to me, but I saw everything I needed to see in his eyes as we said goodbye that evening.

Family and friends gave so much of themselves for J.R. and me. The support system that surrounded us over the years was incredible. There was always someone willing to help us. Regardless of what was going on in their own lives, they centered their lives on the two of us. I knew I could depend on them day and night. I could name those special people, but the list would be too long. I will never forget the love that was shown towards us. I am still very lucky because all of these wonderful people are still looking out for me five years later. I have their love every day. I can depend on them to be there to help when I am having a bad day. Even though years have passed since J.R.'s death, it is comforting for me to know I still have a strong support group of family and friends to lean on.

It is this experience that led me to volunteer at the Hillman Cancer Center. I was unable to make this decision until recently. The beauty of giving is being able to give back to others in need of support and encouragement, while also giving myself the chance to help others as I was helped. Being involved with other cancer patients has been bittersweet for me some days. Yet, this opportunity has given back to me a way to help make a difference. I've lived in their devastated world, but can see how much progress has been made in multiple myeloma and other cancers people must suffer. This is such a positive experience for me. I talk about J.R. with such spirit that it becomes obvious to people how much I loved him. It relays to patients and their families how outside support can be a good thing.

Some of the hardest days of my life were made a little easier because of the love, devotion, and understanding that were shown me by family and friends. I owe a lot to the doctors and medical staff who cared for J.R. over the years. Living through a life-threatening disease cannot be done alone. This is my way now to celebrate J.R.'s life, by helping others with cancer. The gift of love he left me with is now my inspiration to volunteer and dedicate my time at the Hillman Cancer Center.

He will wipe every tear from their eyes.
There won't be any more death. There won't be any grief, crying or
pain, because the first things have disappeared.

Revelation 21:4 *(GOD'S WORD)*

CHAPTER SEVEN

Stripped Away

I GREW UP IN A SMALL TOWN, where we left our doors open and played outside until our parents yelled out the doors to come home. We walked to and from school without a care in the world.

When I was sixteen, I was told a dear friend was missing. Missing?

Groups of people were searching for him, and then his family decided to go look for him at their hunting cabin, concerned that maybe something happened while he was hunting.

They found him, but it wasn't a hunting accident. He had been shot and left there by a new acquaintance that he had invited hunting. What? This doesn't happen in a small town-a wake-up call to all of us. This first taste of evil definitely stripped away a layer of innocence and security. The TV shows in 1984 weren't like what they are now. It was SO disturbing—and still is—that someone could do this.

I still have the baseball glove he had given me.

Looking back, I still can't imagine what his family suffered.

A few years later I was living about an hour away, and I was on the treadmill at our gym. As I was watching the TV, I saw a picture of a woman who looked familiar, and then I saw at the bottom of the screen: "Missing Woman in New Castle, PA."

Of course I checked into it further when I left, only to find out she was living three doors up from my parents, next door to my grandparents' old house. She had been missing for a very long time and was last seen at the local store. The pleas for any answers from her family and friends on the newscast were heart wrenching.

Then one Sunday we were in town having dinner with my family. All of a sudden we heard lots of sirens and commotion.

Hikers had found her body in the quarry. Details horrific. This is still a cold case. Shocking-two murders in a few years in a small home town. People literally stripped away from their loved ones by the hand of another.

I bring this type of loss up because, in addition to the grief of losing this loved one, other aspects are now present: anger, fear, searching for answers, finding forgiveness, finding justice . . .

Fast forward to today—

"Man opens fire at political event in Tucson, AZ-19 shot, 6 killed and several injured . . ."

"24-year-old shoots ex-girlfriend and mother of his 2-year-old in the stomach, kills unborn baby and is found sleeping next to her."

"Family slaughtered in own house and father left to die."

You know I could go on and on. Unbelievable events that sometimes are so unfathomable. My heart goes out to each and every person impacted by these types of senseless acts.

Recently I learned of the story of Morgan Harrington. One night she vanished and all that was found was her purse. Sadly, search efforts led to her remains, discovered on a remote 700-acre farm. I watched her parents' story and crusade on the news, and it touched my heart so profoundly. They have been dedicated not only to keeping Morgan's case alive, with the goal of it being brought to justice, but also to raising safety awareness through their efforts. Morgan's father's and mother's strength and commitment to memorializing her carried such a strong message. Hopefully their story will inspire others who have had to live through such a tragedy.

Liz Harrington, Morgan's mother, used the phrase "from ashes to cinder blocks" as the two of them announced "Morgan Rocks." At Morgan's memorial they started a "gathering of rocks" on Morgan's Bridge at Copeley Road on the North Grounds of the University of Virginia. They have asked people to bring a rock and a prayer to add to the collection and to leave them both there.

The first rock that was placed there was from Skyler, a **blinkoncrime.com** contributor. It was a beautiful, painted slate rock with an image of Anchorage Farm, Tibetan prayer flags and an angel rising to the heavens.

The hand of another may have taken them away but their legacy can live on.

Another tragic but touching story is that of Christina Taylor Green, brought into this world on September 11, 2001 and stripped from her family and friends in the tragedy in Tucson along with several others. I know I won't forget watching them raise the 9/11 banner, which includes the remnants of a 30-foot American flag that survived the 2001 terror attacks, at her funeral. This little girl touched so many lives in her short nine years. I do pray that her spirit and love for her country inspire us, as a country, to strive to continue to make it a better place.

Christina's mother, has written a book called *As Good As She Imagined.* Although I found it emotionally difficult to read as I have a young daughter, I was so touched by her honesty and sheer determination to keep her daughter's memory alive and celebrate the impact Christina made on so many people's lives during her short time on this earth.

Sadly we cannot go back and change the past or bring our loved ones back but we can, as survivors, find the strength to move forward and live our lives in a way that would make our lost loved ones proud. Unfortunately we don't have the power to stop all of the evil that exists but we do have control over our own actions and can spread love and joy to the best of our abilities. We can choose how we want to live and impact that we want to make.

Why can't this world be as good as a nine-year old imagined it to be?

Your word is a lamp for my feet and light for my path.

Psalm 119:105 *(GOD'S WORD)*

Time Goes By

The memoris of
eturn with no
sterday us far
in your min
Mome
remem you want
And those yo
Some good
Othe

CHAPTER EIGHT

Words from the Heart

OFTEN, WRITING POETRY OR JOURNALING is a way for people to articulate or describe the feelings that are so difficult to say. The written word is a tool for healing that is very powerful. I have journaled since I was thirteen and have boxes of journals. I am not sure if I will ever read every one of them again, but writing always provided comfort. Whether it was poetry or just writing my thoughts, it always seemed to help to put in on paper.

I have included some meaningful poems that I thought others might enjoy or just relate to.

Grandma, you were the best
and now that you're at rest

I pray that you are blessed
With all the happiness

You filled my heart with joy and laughter
that will remain ever after

I have tears of love
and not of sorrow

because I know you will be with me
Today, Tomorrow, and the days to follow

I wish you were here
because I love you so dear
I know you will always be near

I Love You Grandma!

Love,
Your Grandaughter, Ciara

CIARA POMERICO KEEFER, AGE 13

For her grandmother when she passed away from renal cancer. Poem read at her funeral on April 5, 2001.

Grandma, I just want you to know that this isn't the end, a good-bye isn't forever.
This is just another "see-you-later" because all of us here are going to heaven.

Dean Pomerico, age 15
For his grandmother when she passed away from renal cancer

In Memory of Dad
———— • ————

Our hearts still ache

The "why's" and "what ifs" still echo

Our prayers of peace

Keep our mind at ease

Our lives changed that day

Forever

Looking for signs and signals to comfort us

But the hurt doesn't go away

Back together with Mom

In a better place

No more hurt, no more pain

Is all we can pray

Holding on to our gratefulness

And fond memories

We must find a way to go on

And carry them in our heart ~ forever.

Joy Kalajainen Johnson, 2004

A Healing Place

There is a place in the woods,

A rock covered with moss.

It is surrounded by some bushes and logs.

I call it my healing place.

I sat there today,

Feeling the warmth of the sun touch my face.

And I thought about the warmth of those who have touched my life;

About the smiles that greet me if I would but smile;

About the one who gently rubs my back;

The one who sits near me when the tears begin to fall;

The ones who hold my hand a little longer

than they need to;

The ones who give me a friendly punch in the arm

and let me know we are connected;

The ones who shine their light.

Little things, ordinary things.

Extraordinary power, healing power.

Anne Lanier

Canton, Michigan

Reprinted with permission from Bereavement Publishing, Inc.

Maybe

Maybe you were meant to go
To where the angels fly;
To finally find that peaceful place
Above the earth's blue sky.

Where calm and warmth and love abide
And pain is gone for good;
Where you can soar like never before
And feel the joy you should.

We mourn your loss so deeply
And wish it were not so,
But maybe here on God's green earth
Wasn't best for you to grow.

The grace of God is yours at last,
Pure peace of mind and soul;
And one day, when we meet again,
I will once again be whole.

Kathie Winkler
Middleburg Heights, Ohio

Reprinted with permission from Bereavement Publishing, Inc.

For All That You Are

---•---

For all of your kindness

For all of your patience

For all of the strength that you have

For all of the strength you have given me

For all of the time you have devoted to us

For all of your goodness

For all of the stability

For all of your understanding

And all of the sharing

For all of the love you've given unconditionally

For all of your support

For being our guardian angel

For all that our family is because of you

For all that I have learned

For all the ways that I've grown

For all of the beautiful memories

For all that I am because of you

For all of it, I thank you

I thank you from the bottom of my heart

For the person that you are

For all that you are

I am so thankful that you are my Mother

For all of it, I love you.

Joy Kalajainen Johnson

Given to her mother on Mother's Day, 2000

Lauri Kalajainen, Joy's sister, read this at their mother's funeral on

April 5, 2001, just one year later.

Somebody Painted the Sky

I looked out in awe, as the evening drew near
Far, in the distance, on high
My soul was uplifted and now I have hope,
Because somebody painted the sky.

Streaks of pure silver; surrounded by blue
With dancing clouds, puffy and white
Appeared to be, especially meant just for me
To see, on this memorable night.

The life I was living had come crashing down;
Someone close to my heart had just died.
Grief and much sorrow had taken their toll;
I lost count of the many tears I cried.

Wandering aimlessly, lost in the darkness,
I felt the world's weight on my head.
Hope, all but vanished, the morning gave no will
To even get out of my bed.

But as twilight was fading, I was drawn to the door
To look at a beautiful sight.
Above me, like magic, sky colors exploded
Making me laugh with delight.

Finding Her Way Home

———————— • ————————

She stares across the ocean
Envisioning a place from long ago
Where did she go
Who has she become

Feeling like a ship
Tossing aimlessly in the waves
No sense of direction
No port in sight

She searches for the beacon
To find her way
Back to the dreams
That have faded over time

Longing for the passion
Wanting to feel alive
And revive the soul
Weathered by this sea

A faint light catches her eye
Could this guide her home
Back to the place
That she had left behind

She holds her breath and starts to steer
Taking a chance on this light
Filled with fear and excitement
The path feels right

As she nears, a sense of comfort
Gives her the strength to continue
Suddenly realizing she was not lost
Just fearful of finding her way

The port is now in sight
She sees those dreams again
With a new illumination
Taking on a reality close enough to
grasp

She decides not to look back
Feeling renewed strength
As she is reminded of who she is
And all she wants to become

Joy Kalajainen Johnson

I am convinced that nothing can ever separate us from God's love which Christ Jesus our Lord shows us. We can't be separated by death or life, by angels or rulers, by anything in the present or anything in the future, by forces or powers in the world above or in the world below, or by anything else in creation.

Romans 8:38-39 *(GOD'S WORD)*

CHAPTER NINE
Moving Forward

So MUCH EASIER SAID THAN DONE. I received an email from a lovely friend in Spain letting us know about the passing of her dear "mum." We were working together when I lost both of my parents, and she was actually with me when I got the message about the loss of my father. It's hard to be so far away from someone when they are grieving and you just want to give them a hug and be there for them.

She commented that she was sitting there in a fog. . .

I know that fog so well. Although it has been several years now since I lost my parents, I remember those times, the emptiness and the pain, like it was yesterday. I am so blessed to have a wonderful husband, six amazing stepchildren in addition to my beautiful little girl, and a great extended family. I am blessed that my parents and God gave me the strength to move forward. I miss them every day, but they are with me in my heart and soul.

If you have lost a loved one, my hope is that you aim to find peace and consciously allow yourself to make the journey. My hope is that you find ways to remember while still living your life. It's a difficult balance, I know, and some days you will feel as confident as a tightrope walker and the next day as vulnerable as an infant learning to walk.

If you haven't found out already, you will probably experience many different reactions from loved ones and friends-some will surprise you by pulling away, while others will comfort you and be your rock. It can be a lonely road, though, as no one really knows your thoughts and feelings. People can empathize, but, in the end, no one's loss is exactly like another's. The common thread is that we all grieve-just in our own ways.

Remember, no one but ourselves allows us to reach inside and find the strength to move forward. A support network sure makes it a lot easier, but we each need to find those tiny or large steps with our unique footprint. Find ways to remember, to carry on their memory, fight for a cure and continue their legacy. Research the many resources available to see what may be able to help guide or comfort you.

I have faulted and stumbled in my journey, getting caught up in my own life as a refuge and sometimes wanting to stay in a bubble. I have to remind myself that these experiences are to make you stronger. Hopefully you will write your story in your own way. Remember to love with all of your heart and allow yourself to have the good days and the bad. It's OK to have a complete break down at a song or a memory and when you least expect it. Some of the emptiness may never go away. In a way, though, to me that's OK. I don't want to forget the pain of being without my loved ones as it also reminds me how precious every day is.

I re-read the passages from Mom's and Dad's funerals often, but there is one thing my uncle, David McConahy, shared about my mom that I love to read again and again . . . *"I will always remember her loving kindness and, even though we have become less by her passing, there is great reunion and rejoicing in Heaven this day. The last time I saw her she said, 'I'm going to Heaven' and 'I love you.' I can think of no way to improve upon those words."*

I am so thankful that he shared this. Knowing the strength of her faith comforts me every day.

Just remember: it wouldn't be this hard if we hadn't had the opportunity to love and be loved.

My four-year-old daughter asked me last night out of the blue, "Mommy, do you miss your mommy?" I told her, "Absolutely, every day" as I welled up a bit. Then she said, "Do you miss your Daddy too?"

"Yes, I do. I wish every day that they could be here with us — they would have so much fun with you." She hugged me and said, "I'm sorry they aren't here with you, but they are probably happy in Heaven."

How insightful. All I could do was hug her back, saying "Yes, I am sure they are very happy in Heaven" as I fought back the tears.

Prayer Song

We light a candle and say a prayer
Expect to see their faces but they're not there
Fallen Americans for them we pray
Goodbye and so much more we meant to say

So we cry tears of hope for better days
Make this heartache go away so these sad times can end
So we cry Lord let Your light shine down its rays
Save us from the fire's blaze
Help us all to find a way to live in peace amen

There's no denying they feel the pain
Sometimes their sunny days just turn to rain
They miss their precious smiles and loving eyes
They try to understand the reasons why

So they cry tears of hope for better days
Make this heartache go away so these sad times can end
So they cry Lord let Your light shine down its rays
End the hatred calm the rage
Help us all to find a way to live in peace amen

Now time is passing seasons have changed
Wish there was some way we could have them back again
God bless these weary souls comfort our hearts
They all live on in us though we must part

So we cry tears of hope for better days
Make this heartache go away so these sad times can end
So we cry Lord let Your light shine down its rays
Guide us as we live each day
Help us all to find a way to live in peace amen
Help us all to find a way to live in peace amen

Words and music by George Johnson

For the victims of 9/11, their families, and those who have lost loved ones
in Iraq and Afghanistan, and all those who have sacrificed for our freedom.

So You Dance

There on the ledge of despair and denial
Watching your world fall apart
Lost and confused like your faith is on trial
Longing for something to comfort your heart

Hearing the news that your daddy is dying
Getting that call on that day
Photos of him still alive leave you crying
Feeling like part of you faded away

So you dance to the music move with the changes
Dance to a new favorite groove
Dance to the love songs that life rearranges
Just take a chance and your hopes and your dreams may come true

Facing the feelings inside you
You're praying for your peace of mind
Releasing the past far behind you
'Hoping to make up for lost precious time

Watching the sunrise above the blue ocean
Breathing the mist from the waves
The tide keeps on changing the world is in motion
Your passion for living your life has been saved

So you dance to the music move with the changes
Dance to a new favorite groove
Dance to the love songs that life rearranges
Just take a chance and your hopes and your dreams may come true

Words and Music by George Johnson

To My Mom

To my Mom a thank you song
For all you have given to me
For taking good care of our family
For loving me unconditionally
I thank you with all of my heart

If this were a letter I would want it to say
Dear Mom I love you and hope you are happy today
I miss you especially when you're far away
For all you have given I can never repay

To my Mom a thank you song
For all you have given to me
For taking good care of our family
For loving me unconditionally
I thank you with all of my heart

If this were a prayer on my knees I would pray
Dear Lord please watch over my mother today
Please bring her some sunshine when her skies are gray
Your grace is her comfort and your light guides her way

To my Mom a thank you song
For all you have given to me
For taking good care of our family
For loving me unconditionally
I thank you with all of my heart
I thank you with all of my heart
I thank you with all of my heart

Words and music by George Johnson

Then young women will rejoice and dance along with young men and old men.
I will turn their mourning into joy. I will comfort them
I will give them joy in place of their sorrow.

Jeremiah 31:13 *(GOD'S WORD)*